Can I tell you about Sensory Processing Difficulties?

Can I tell you about...?

The 'Can I tell you about...?' series offers simple introductions to a range of limiting conditions and other issues that affect our lives. Friendly characters invite readers to learn about their experiences, the challenges they face, and how they would like to be helped and supported. These books serve as excellent starting points for family and classroom discussions.

Other subjects covered in the Can I tell you about...? series

ADHD

Adoption

Anxiety

Asperger Syndrome

Asthma

Autism

Cerebral Palsy

Dementia

Depression

Diabetes (Type 1)

Down Syndrome

Dyslexia

Dyspraxia

Eating Disorders

Eczema

Epilepsy

ME/Chronic Fatigue Syndrome

Nut Allergy

OCD

Parkinson's Disease

Pathological Demand Avoidance Syndrome

Peanut Allergy

Selective Mutism

Stammering/Stuttering

Stroke

Tourette Syndrome

Can I tell you about Sensory Processing Difficulties?

A guide for friends, family and professionals

SUE ALLEN
Illustrated by Mike Medaglia

Jessica Kingsley *Publishers*
London and Philadelphia

First published in 2016
by Jessica Kingsley Publishers
73 Collier Street
London N1 9BE, UK
and
400 Market Street, Suite 400
Philadelphia, PA 19106, USA

www.jkp.com

Library of Congress Cataloging in Publication Data
Allen, Sue (Psychotherapist)
Can I tell you about sensory processing difficulties?: a guide for friends, family and professionals / Sue Allen.
pages cm.--(Can I tell you about...?)
Audience: Age 5-11.
Includes bibliographical references and index.

ISBN 978-1-84905-640-3 (alk. paper)

1. Sensory integration dysfunction in children--Juvenile literature.
2. Sensory disorders in children--Juvenile literature. I. Title.

RJ496.S44A45 2016
618.92'8--dc23
2015015997s

British Library Cataloguing in Publication Data
A CIP catalogue record for this book is available from the British Library

ISBN 978 1 84905 640 3
eISBN 978 1 78450 137 2

Printed and bound in Great Britain

Acknowledgements

Thanks to all the children and families who share their everyday challenges and successes. To the Sensory Integration Network (UK and Ireland) team past and present. Thanks also to Sarah Wink and Jane Allen for encouragement and feedback on this project. Understanding sensory processing changes lives.

Contents

Preface

This book is for children aged 5 to 11 years and their parents and teachers. It provides a basic introduction to sensory processing difficulties.

All of us process sensory information and perceive the world in subtly different ways. This book provides a beginner's guide to sensory processing difficulties and some of the things that can make life easier for children and families. Focus on the sections that are useful to you. Our understanding in this area is rapidly developing and further reading is suggested at the back of the book.

"Hi, my name is Harry and this is my sister Anna; we have Sensory Processing Difficulties."

"Hi. My name is Harry and I have sensory processing difficulties. Some people call it SPD and others call it sensory integration difficulties. Seeing, hearing, touching and smelling tell us about the world around us. Movement, muscles senses, stretch and touch on our inside tells us about how our body is working and moving. Senses help us to know where we are, to know what to do and how to do it. For me those messages get in a muddle. This makes it tricky to pay attention, do my school work and even play with my friends. To me it can be annoying; but there are ways that I can make everyday life easier and more fun.

Sometimes I feel like my senses are crowding in on me and sound is too loud, touch is too scratchy, and lights are too bright. This makes me feel stressed. I just want to go somewhere quiet and not talk to anyone.

My sister is called Anna. She has some sensory processing difficulties too. She misses what people say or her hands don't tell her what they are touching or holding. Teachers can get cross because they think she is not listening when she is really trying. She has to look at her hands to know what they are doing.

It helps us both to do warm-up exercises (like bouncing on a mini trampoline) before we have to pay attention, do school work or even get dressed or go to sleep."

"Our dog Patches likes it when I scratch between his ears; it suits me not to touch his fur too much as light or tickly things bother me."

"The feeling of my nails being cut is horrible. It helps to have a massage or a hug from Mum first. Other things that bother my skin are clothes labels or seams, or tickly things. I like clothes that are soft but sometimes it is easier to wear clothes that are really tight so they don't move on my skin. When I am eating I hate slimy stuff in my mouth. I like to eat things that are crunchy, hard or chewy. Sometimes I like to crunch ice or drink a shake or smoothie through a big straw. It helps my mouth get ready for other food.

Anna says 'When I try to make a model I know how to build it but my hands don't seem to do as they are told. It is hard to pick up small pieces and keep a hold that is not too tight or too soft. I have to be very careful if I hold something fragile in my hands because sometimes I squeeze too hard and it breaks.'

You can help by listening when I tell you or show you that I am bothered. Firm but gentle touch or massage on my hands or back can help. It's also good to do this or some stretches before I use my hands.

When eating, washing or dressing is a problem it's probably best to find an Occupational Therapist or Speech Therapist to help out."

"It helps to carry something heavy and wear a baseball cap and sunglasses."

"Sometimes bright lights bother me. I don't like going to the supermarket because the lights flicker. It helps to wear a baseball cap and sunglasses. At school I like to sit near the front of the class so people don't walk in front of me when I am looking at the teacher. When I am doing school work I like to be in a shady spot. It's hard for me to pay attention when it's too bright or too dark.

Sometimes it's hard for my eyes to stay in one place. It helps to use a ruler or bookmark or to follow my finger when I am reading.

My eyes help me to see and work out where to go and what is going to happen next, especially when I am moving. It helps to have a clear view of where I am going, without too many other people walking by. My teacher lets me go to the canteen before everyone else so I don't have to walk down a busy corridor.

Lots of us get tired eyes, when we spend too much time on screens. I give my eyes a break by going outside to play or looking out of the window.

It's always good to see an optician regularly. Some people find it's useful to see a Behavioural Optometrist. Coloured lenses or eye exercises help some people."

"Sometimes songs or clapping a rhythm help Anna to organise her movements. Sound helps her to know where she is and music with a good beat helps her to move better."

"It is important that our hearing helps us know about danger. Sometimes our hearing is too sensitive and tells us there is danger when there is not.

I hate really loud sounds like the school bell, hand dryers or people shouting. I feel sick inside and want to run away. I use ear defenders that look like headphones. Instead of having music they help make things quieter. Then I can feel calmer and pay attention. At night time when I try to go to sleep it helps to listen to a story tape or the sound of waves.

Hearing works with our movement sense to tell us where noise comes from and what is making the noise. This helps us to make a map inside our head of the world around us.

Hearing is very important in understanding what people say but also the way that they say it. Think about the different ways that you can say the same word and how it changes what that word means. Choose any word, like 'thank you', and see how many different ways you can make it sound.

Hearing is quite complicated and when it's not working well it can make everyday life a challenge. Audiologists, Speech and Language Therapists and Occupational Therapists can help by working out what's going on. They will look at how to help, from using soundproofing to reduce background noise, to playing movement games, to computer games or special music."

"Sometimes smells that other people think are OK are horrible for me. It can help me to suck on a straw or chew something."

"Smell helps us to find good things like tasty food. It also helps us to stay away from things that are not good for us like food that has gone bad.

Smell also helps me to know if things are good or bad. Sometimes smells that don't bother other people are horrible for me. I hate it when anyone wears perfume or the smell of the lunch hall at school – yeuch! If I am going somewhere that I know will have a smell I don't like I will take a lolly to suck or gum to chew. Sometimes I use a tissue with a smell I like to cover my nose. This helps to block out the bad smells.

Taste helps me know if things are good to eat or not. It can take me a lot of tastes to like a new food. Eating chewy or crunchy foods helps to get my mouth ready before I eat something new, then new foods don't feel so strange in my mouth.

Anna does not always notice smell or tastes. When she eats her food she likes to add loads of chilli sauce. Anna likes lots of different foods. I like to stick to the same foods but my parents encourage me to try new things. It helps me to take new foods very slowly."

"I like to play tug of war before we sit down for dinner because it helps me stay sitting on my chair."

"Our body sense is really important to help us feel OK but most people never notice it. My body tells me where it is from the feeling I get when my muscles and joints move. The more I move or do hard muscle work the more I feel where my body is.

It can be really tough to sit still because my body forgets where it is. Sitting on a ball chair or wobble cushion can help because I can move a little bit without anyone else noticing. If I have to sit on a chair it helps to push on the chair through my arms just to get a reminder as to where my body is.

Knowing where my body is also really helps when I am doing sport. When I play catch, it helps to do warm-up exercises like jumping on the spot and trying to push the wall down with my arms. This helps my hands to be in the right place at the right time to catch the ball.

My favourite sports are ones that make my muscles work hard like climbing and trampolining. Some days Anna and I make an obstacle course around the lounge with blankets and cushions. It's so cool to do I don't mind helping to clear up afterwards!"

"Sometimes I feel like an astronaut lost in space – I don't know which way is up! I like it best when my feet are on the ground."

"Moving helps us to know where we are and how our bodies work. It tells us about danger and if we might fall over. It also helps us to learn about how other people or things can move. Understanding our own bodies helps us to control the world around us.

Movements that other people find OK can be scary for me. I hate having my hair washed in the bath because I have to tip my head back. It feels like I am going to fall over and knock myself out. Moving in a straight line, like bouncing on a trampoline or going on a straight slide, feels good but corners or bends just make me feel dizzy. When we go on a car ride I push my legs against the chair in front, I put my hands on my head and push down and I look out of the window. This helps me keep my brain together.

Anna took ages to learn to ride her bike. She said balancing and using the pedals at the same time was confusing. She went to Occupational Therapy and did lots of swinging, climbing and obstacle courses. Now she's better than me at riding a bike. She says now she wants to ride a horse."

"The quiet corner can help me stay in control."

"When too much sensation is coming into my brain I get cross. When I feel like that, it's difficult for me to stay in control; I feel like shouting, running away, hitting out or curling up into a ball. It's hard for me to tell people how I feel or to listen to what people are saying to me. At school there is a quiet corner in a tent with beanbags. Sometimes I need adults to help me do some breathing to calm down."

TOUCH

"Sometimes the touch of clothes bothers me. I hate having trousers on because of the feeling of the waistband and the seams on socks are scratchy. It helps if I jump up and down or jump on the trampoline before I have to put my socks on. When I have a bath it helps to wrap up in a towel and have my back, hands and feet rubbed. This helps make the bedsheets feel all right. I also like the weight of heavy blankets to help me go to sleep."

"It helps me to go to sleep at night if the lights are soft and I have a heavy blanket. My fan keeps me cool and helps to stop noise from outside."

MOVEMENT

"It's good to move but sometimes it's too much. I went to the park and went on the swing, and my friend made it go high. To start with it was OK but then I felt gross and wobbly. For a while after that I felt scared to go to the park. Dad helped me to get used to it again; we went when the park was quiet and I just leaned on the swing on my tummy. When that felt OK I sat on and pushed it a bit with my feet, but kept my feet on the ground. I still don't like going on it when there are other kids around but I am getting better all the time."

SOUND

"Most people can ignore sound that bothers them, but for me it's tricky. I can hear what's going on in the next room and the next room after that. If somebody is banging their pencil on the table it sounds like an invasion of elephants! Sometimes going somewhere quiet helps; other times I use my ear defenders. It can also help to have a constant background noise like a fan. It helps me when other people don't talk too much or just talk quietly."

VISION

"It makes it hard to sleep if I watch TV or play computer games before bedtime. My parents say the blue light wakes my brain up too much so I avoid screens for an hour or two before bed."

"It's good to do exercise every day. Balance can be hard but we are getting better the more we do. We like to practise our judo with Dad."

Anna says:

TOUCH

"Things often fall out of my hand when I try to hold them (like my pencil). It helps to use a heavy pen so that I can feel it better. I was quite slow learning to write because I had to watch what my hand was doing more than other people but it's getting better. I like using a computer because then it's easier to read my writing. Waking up my muscles by doing warm-up exercises helps too. My favourite is wheelbarrow walking!"

MOVEMENT

"Sports can be tricky. I know it's good to do exercise every day. My favourite activity at the playground is the slide and I also like tap dancing, running and martial arts. These activities make me know where I am and help me to feel more organised. I help Dad to dig his vegetable patch. Carrying the watering can is difficult because it's heavy but I can feel my muscles getting stronger."

SOUND

"I get told off for not listening, but I just don't know that people have said anything, especially if the TV is on. Its helps me if you gently touch my shoulder or go where I can see you; that reminds me to pay attention and listen. Using rhythm can help me find it easier to listen."

TASTE

"I like food with lots of taste like curry or chilli! Food tastes better to me with ketchup or mustard. I try to remember to chew the food to get the flavour."

SENSORY OVER RESPONSIVE (SOR)

"This is when too much sensory information is coming into our brains. It is stressful and can be overwhelming. When we have SOR it's difficult to listen, concentrate or pay attention. It can make us anxious or struggle to behave in a way others would want, or expect us to."

SENSORY UNDER RESPONSIVENESS (SUR)

"This is when too little sensory information is reaching the brain. SUR can make it difficult to be interested or pay attention, to organise movement, play or work projects; or to be fast enough in doing things."

SENSORY SEEKING (SS)

"Sometimes when too little or too much information is reaching the brain we are seeking more sensation. This can be through movement, e.g. rocking or being always on the move. It can be though touching (e.g. touching ourselves, other people or things). SS can also lead to excessive tasting, smelling and looking."

"Using my muscles helps me."

"Sensory 'snacks' are activities that we can do to help us feel calm, alert and organised. The best thing for me to feel good is making my muscles work hard. This helps all my other senses feel more organised. My muscles work hard when I push, pull, stretch, lift or carry.

Anna and I do some games together to help us get ready in the morning.

I am very bouncy when I wake up in the morning. Anna can be a bit grumpy."

THINGS I LIKE

"These are all good sensory 'snacks':

- Pillow fights – Mum doesn't mind as long as we only use the pillows below our shoulders.
- Trampoline – when the weather is OK we get to go out to the yard and take it in turns to have a bounce.
- Toothbrush time – Anna likes an electric toothbrush but I don't like the feel of it. It helps me if I pull monster faces to stretch my muscles, then the feel of the toothbrush is OK.

- Wall push-ups – before breakfast we have a competition to see who can do the most standing-up wall press-ups in 30 seconds.

- Music – on the school bus I like to listen to music, Anna talks to her friend.

- Breaktime/recess – after sitting still in class it's great to get the chance to run around at recess. Sometimes Anna says she's too tired from sitting still. I agree sitting still can be really hard work.

- Food snacks – I like chewy or crunchy foods. Drinking thick drinks through a straw or cold drinks can be very calming and organising. Chewing gum is good for me but I can only have it when mum says it's OK.

- Playground – after school we go to the park most days.
- Homework – Anna likes to do her homework sitting at the table. I like to be standing up or even better walking around.
- Bedtime – I always like to have a shower before I go to bed, Anna likes to have a bath. I like heavy bedcovers, Anna likes a duvet. I like to listen to a story or music, Anna likes to read. I like the window closed and the fan on. Anna likes the windows open. I like the lights out, Anna has a night light. My parents say we have individual sensory preferences but that helps us all get a good night's sleep.

At school:

- Using a rubber strip (like Theraband) around chair legs lets me fidget with my feet without disturbing anyone else.
- Quiet area – I like snuggling under the bean bags, I used to use it quite a lot but now it's only occasionally. I have a card I can give my teacher if I feel like I need some quiet time. Sometimes I go there with a few others to do school work that needs me to listen and concentrate."

How parents can help

Everybody's sensory preferences are unique to them. No one else can tell you how you feel inside but your nonverbal communication will give other people clues. First of all think about how you look and feel when you are happy and relaxed or stressed or angry. Then think about how you recognise that in other people and your child. Practise reading those cues and thinking what the sensory qualities of that experience or environment are.

UNDERSTAND

Sensory processing difficulties cause stress to children and to their families. They make the things that we do every day more challenging. They are hard for other people to see and understand. Help friends and family to understand either by giving them books or websites to read or by going to a talk with them.

CHANGE THE ENVIRONMENT

If sound, vision, touch or movement in the environment is causing stress, consider reducing the stimulus within the environment; for example, turn down sound, go to a quiet space, pull down the blinds, use a dimmer switch on lights. If children are having difficulty picking up on sensory information use heavy resistance games to help 'switch on' their muscles and sensory processing pathways. Activities that involve pushing, pulling, carrying or lifting are great for working the major muscle groups and this is the safest strategy for helping children to be ready for action. Day-to-day activities that can help include: climbing, swinging and slides, cycling, swimming, obstacle courses, large-scale construction, push-ups (can be on a wall or chair), gardening or yard work, polishing or sweeping, helping carry shopping. Encourage your child to tell you about sensory stimuli that help them feel calm, for example smell, music, dancing or watching a bubble tube or waves.

CHANGE THE ACTIVITY

If you think an activity will be challenging for a child, start with a warm-up exercise, for example pushing against flat hands or jumping on the spot. Try to break the task down into smaller steps.

WHEN TO ASK FOR HELP

If sensory processing difficulties are getting in the way of the activities that your child wants or needs to do every day it's a good idea to ask for help (see 'More help' below).

How teachers can help

UNDERSTAND

- All of us have different sensory preferences and tolerance levels for sensory information. This will impact on children's learning styles. Games that involve only visual demonstration or only verbal instructions (e.g. copying a sequence of movements versus 'Simon says') will give you a starting point to identify their preferred or best learning strategies. Encourage children to be aware of what works best for them but also to practise different strategies.
- A busy classroom environment can be overwhelming for children with sensory processing difficulties. Those who over-respond to sensory information are likely to have increasing difficulty as the day and week progresses, showing signs of tiredness or stress. Look out for children who demonstrate fight or flight responses to sound, visual, touch or even movement stimulus. This may include covering ears or hiding when a bell goes, or hitting out when brushed against by other children. They may avoid sports, especially when feet are away from the ground or backward or rotational movement is required.

- Under-responders appear switched off or do not appear to notice stimulus; they may not notice that clothes are twisted on their body, or food is on their face, or balance may be a challenge. These children are most often missed, as they are seen as well behaved, but they can also make the most progress when offered the right sensory input.

CHANGE THE ENVIRONMENT

- Light. Is your classroom lighting comfortable for everyone? Lights that flicker can cause stress, for example halogen lighting may be preferable to fluorescent strip lighting. Can you decrease or increase lighting levels according to the activity level required? Visual movement or seeing people move while you are trying to pay attention is particularly disruptive to some children. You may wish to think about layout so that children who struggle with visual attention do not have to deal with others walking in front of them. Visually busy walls (with lots of pictures or posters) can also be very visually distracting. You might want to think about keeping one wall in your classroom blank.

- Sound. Sound-absorbing materials or quiet spaces can help over-responders. Also consider background noise and where possible consider reducing it when focused attention on instructions is required. Under-responders will benefit from cueing into the need to listen. You might want to mark transitions, for example with use of colour on a screen or gesture cues.

- Smell. What does your classroom smell like? Are any children bothered by the smell? Look for scrunched-up noses! Then check the chapter on taste and smell for ideas.

CHANGE THE ACTIVITY

- Physical warm-ups (e.g. jumping on the spot, pushing down on chair or table, star jumps, handshakes) increase body awareness (proprioception). This helps focus attention and organise body movements. A good time to use strategies like this is before sitting, before writing or before listening.

- When two senses are paired we tend to learn better, for example exploring number cut-outs with our hands combines touch and movement. Copying actions uses vision and movement. It is normal when learning a new skill such as handwriting to watch very closely what your hands are doing – however, as the skill gets more refined and to help us increase speed, the need for close vision is dropped in favour of faster systems such as body awareness (also known as proprioception). Practise new activities with different sensory systems, for example when learning numbers, look, feel and draw on skin (with a finger rather than a pen) then move through the shape.

- For children with sensory processing challenges, enriching sensory feedback is often helpful. However, cognitive strategies involving goal setting and talking themselves through a challenge can also help (verbal self-guidance). Where you can, ask a question rather than providing an answer; in this way the child practises problem solving and planning. Doing as you are told engages small parts of the brain. Planning to reach a goal, with or without support, engages many parts of the brain and provides richer active learning opportunities.

More help

Children with sensory processing difficulties face challenges to participation in everyday life. If you think that your child or student is struggling then further assessment is recommended. Treatment may address a variety of areas needed for daily functioning, for example washing, dressing, toileting, bathing, mealtimes, movement, play, school skills, paying attention, sitting or standing still, regulating emotional responses, communicating, organising and planning.

PEOPLE WHO CAN HELP

- Occupational Therapists (OTs) help individuals and their families to be successful in their daily activities, for example self-care, work or school skills, rest and play.
- Physiotherapists (PTs) promote mobility and related function.
- Speech and Language Therapists (SLTs) promote communication and language skills, and a specialist will look at social interaction or feeding.
- Community or Developmental Paediatricians – these are doctors who specialise in working with children who are experiencing developmental challenges.

- Opticians assess and treat visual difficulties.
- Orthoptists help people with difficulty with eye movements or making both eyes work together.
- Audiologists assess and treat hearing and balance.

Professionals will ask and consider: what is the issue and how can we improve the quality of life for the child and family?

First, assessment: diagnosis of sensory processing difficulties is best identified by an OT, PT or SLT with postgraduate training in Sensory Integration. Many children will also benefit from assessment by a Community Paediatrician who can exclude another diagnosis. Some will benefit from assessment by an Educational Psychologist to identify strategies to support learning.

There are several ways to help sensory processing difficulties; including Sensory Integration Therapy, sensory strategies (also known as sensory snacks or a sensory diet) and consultation:

- Ayres Sensory Integration Therapy (ASI) was initially developed by an OT and psychologist called Jean Ayres. This is a play-based approach to improving underlying sensory processing with the aim of improving daily occupations, from brushing your teeth to sitting in class at school. It requires a play environment that offers a variety of touch, body awareness and movement opportunities that are physically and emotionally safe and extend the child's range of skills in a supportive manner. It is preferred that therapists have received postgraduate training, have appropriate supervision and work with parents. Where possible they will also work with the child to set goals that help them participate more in daily life.

- Sensory strategies or a sensory diet: after careful assessment your therapist may provide specific activities to use that will help your child cope better with everyday life. This may be in the form of exercises or may involve equipment, for example a ball chair, wobble cushion or weighted equipment. Response to equipment is highly variable. Some children make great improvements whilst others do not. For this reason it is important to monitor change and keep use of equipment under review.
- Consultation: parents and therapists may work together to problem solve challenges in daily life.

SOME FACTS

- All of us have differences in the way that we process sensory information. For some it is an easy, automatic process that we never have to think about. For others it makes understanding and interacting with the world a challenge.
- About 5 to 15 per cent of preschoolers present with difficulties in processing and integrating sensory information.[1]
- Sensory processing difficulties can be seen on their own, but are more commonly seen with another diagnosis.[2]
- About 70 to 90 per cent of people with Autistic Spectrum conditions have some difficulties with sensory processing.[3]
- Rates of sensory processing difficulties in those with attention deficit and hyperactivity disorder as well as those with developmental coordination disorders are higher than would be expected in the typical population.[4]

1 Ahn, R.R., Miller, L.J., Millberger, S. and McIntosh, D.M. (2004) 'Prevalence of parents' perceptions of sensory processing disorders among kindergarten children.' *American Journal of Occupational Therapy 58*, 287 293. doi:10.5014/ajot.58.3.287

2 Reynolds, S. and Lane, S.J. (2008) 'Diagnostic validity of sensory over-responsivity: a review of the literature and case reports.' *Journal of Autism and Developmental Disorders 38*, 3, 516–529.

3 Adamson, A., O'Hare, A. and Graham, C. (2006) 'Impairments in sensory modulation in children with Autistic Spectrum Disorder.' *British Journal of Occupational Therapy 69*, 8, 357–364.

4 Miller, L.J. (2014) Sensational Kids: Hope and Help for Children with Sensory Processing Disorder (SPD), revised edition. New York: Perigree Books. Zwicker, J.G., Missiuna, C., Harris, S.R. and Boyd, L.A. (2012) 'Developmental coordination disorder: a review and update.' *European Journal of Paediatric Neurology 16*, 6, 573–581.

- Our understanding of sensory processing across the lifespan has been developing for nearly 50 years. It continues to develop rapidly as our ability to understand the brain and its influence on learning and behaviour increases. Case studies have reported difficulties in all age groups but also that treatment can have an impact at any age. Adults are often better at adjusting their life to make things easier but can experience the same issues.

Recommended reading, organisations and websites

BOOKS FOR CHILDREN AND YOUNG ADULTS

Farrington Wilson, L. (2010) *Squirmy Wormy: How I Learned to Help Myself.* Arlington: Future Horizons.

A picture book to share for young children about autism and sensory processing.

Harris, A. and Oberholster, N. (2010) *Mathilda has Touch Sensitivity.* Kirby-in-Ashfield: Special Direct.

A story about tactile defensiveness for children.

Henry, D. (2004) *Tools for Teens.* Flagstaff, AZ: HenryOT.

A great resource for teens and their families to help understand sensory processing and identify practical strategies for daily life.

O'Sullivan, N. (2014) *I'll Tell You Why ...I Can't Wear Those Clothes.* London: Jessica Kingsley Publishers.

An interactive book to help children with tactile defensiveness and their families.

BOOKS FOR TEACHERS, PARENTS AND THERAPISTS

Anderson, J.M. (1998) *Sensory Motor Issues in Autism.* San Antonio: Therapy Skill Builders.

A useful book for considering the child's environment – very practical.

Ayres, A.J. (2005) *Sensory Integration and the Child – 25th Anniversary Edition.* Los Angeles, CA: Western Psychological Services

An update of A. Jean Ayres' original book for parents and teachers.

Dunn, W. (2009) *Living Sensationally: Understanding Your Senses.* London: Jessica Kingsley Publishers.

This is a unique book that helps adults identify their own sensory processing preferences and use that information to enhance their relationships and daily life. Some parents report that this book has changed their life.

Kranowitz, C. (2005) *The Out of Sync Child.* New York: Perigee.

Written by a preschool teacher to help parents, teachers and non-OTs to help recognise and cope with sensory pressing disorder.

Miller, L. (2007) *Sensational Kids: Hope and Help for Children with Sensory Processing Disorders.* New York: Perigee.

This book provides information on background, types of dysfunction and practical strategies with a summary of research. A helpful book for parents.

YOUTUBE VIDEOS

What is Sensory Processing Disorder?
www.youtube.com/watch?v=6O6CmOWxEZA

A stickman cartoon that helps explain challenges in sensory processing.

A Child's View of Sensory Processing
www.youtube.com/watch?v=D1G5ssZlVUw

ORGANISATIONS

UK and Ireland

SINetwork
SI Network (UK & Ireland) Ltd
27A High Street
Theale
RG7 5AH
Phone: UK +44 (0)118 324 1588, Ireland +353 (0)76 680 1580
Fax: +44 (0)118 324 0310
Email: support@sensoryintegration.org.uk
Website: www.sensoryintegration.org.uk

The SI Network (UK and Ireland) is a not-for-profit organisation, promoting education, good practice and research into the theory and practice of Ayres' Sensory Integration.

USA

Sensory Integration Global Network
Contact through the website
Website: www.siglobalnetwork.org

SIGN is made up of a group of volunteers who are dedicated to protecting the integrity and promoting the work of Dr. A. Jean Ayres in Sensory Integration Theory and Intervention.

SPD Foundation
Contact through the website
5420 S. Quebec Street, Suite 135
Greenwood Village, CO 80111
Phone: 303.794.1182
Fax: 303.322.5550
Website: www.spdfoundation.net

The SPD Foundation promotes research, education and awareness for Sensory Processing Disorder.

South Africa

South African Institute for Sensory Integration (SAISI)
P.O. Box 14510 Hatfield Pretoria South Africa 0028
Phone: 012 362 5457
Fax: 086 652 3658
Email: saisi@uitweb.co.za
Website: www.instsi.co.za

This organisation aims to provide training and education in Ayres' Sensory Integration.

Blank for your notes

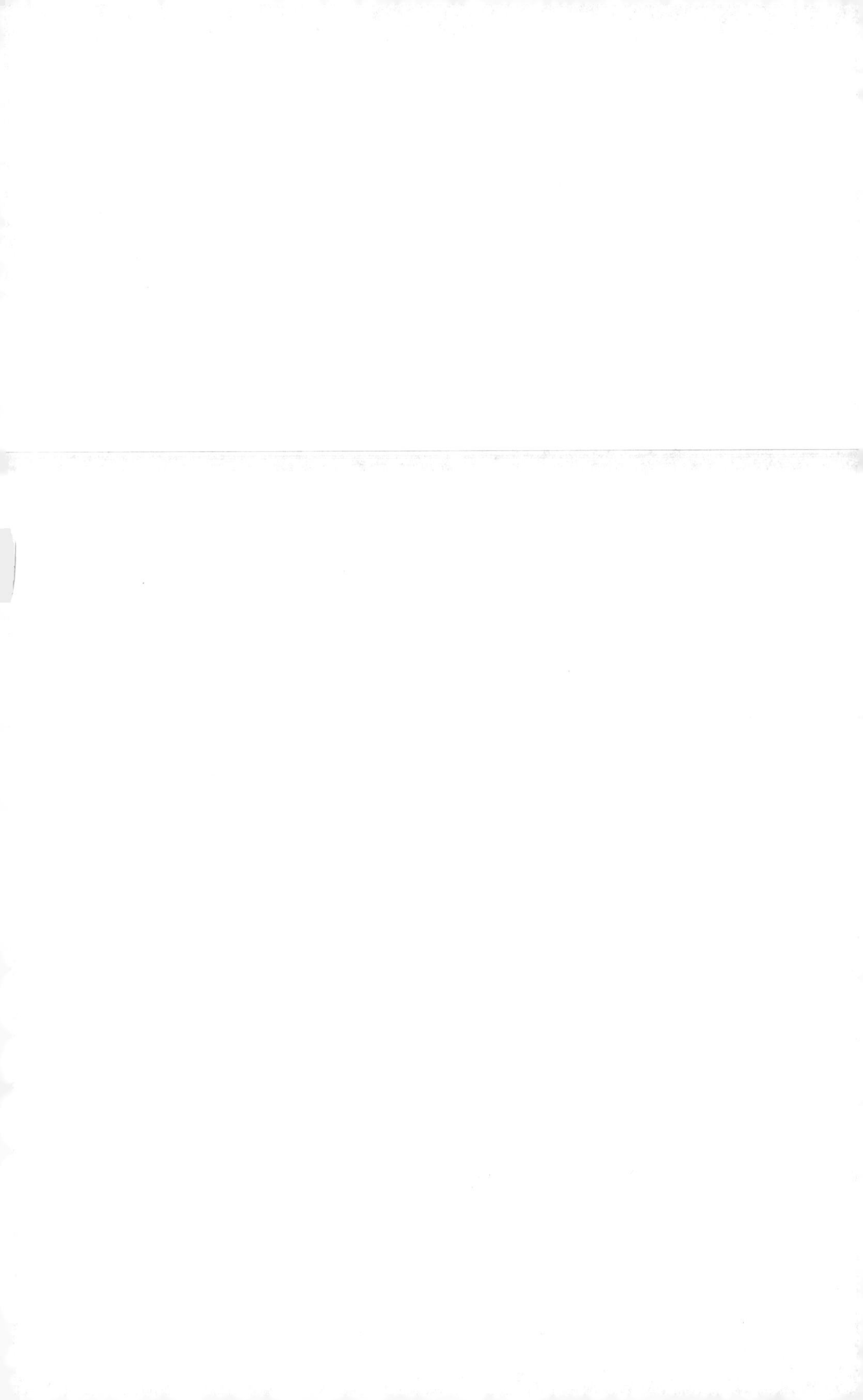